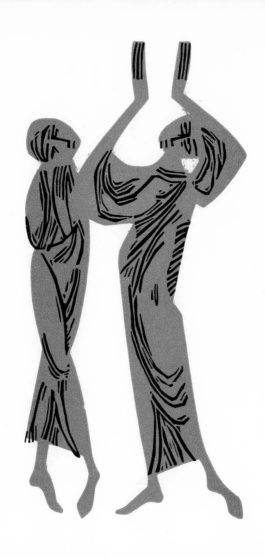

# LITTLE
# BOOK
# OF
# PRAYERS

• • •

ILLUSTRATED
BY JEFF HILL
FOR THE
PETER
PAUPER PRESS

MOUNT VERNON
NEW YORK

# LITTLE
# BOOK
# OF
# PRAYERS

● ●

STRENGTHEN me, O God, by the grace of Thy Holy Spirit; grant me to be strengthened with might in the inner man, and to put away from my heart all useless anxiety and distress, and let me never be drawn aside by various longings after anything whatever, whether it be worthless or precious; but may I regard all things as passing away, and myself as passing away with them.

For nothing is lasting under the sun, for all things are vanity and vexation of spirit. O, how wise is he who thus regards them.

Grant me, O Lord, heavenly wisdom, that I may learn to seek Thee above all things, and to understand all other things as they are, according to the order of Thy wisdom.

Grant me prudently to avoid the one who flatters me, and patiently to bear with the one who contradicts me; for it is a mark of great wisdom not to be moved by every wind of words, nor to give ear to the wicked flattery of the siren; for thus we shall go on securely in the course we have begun. *Thomas à Kempis*

O LORD, Thou lover of souls, in whose hand is the life of every living thing, we bring before Thee in our prayers all those who are lonely in the world. Thine they are, and none can pluck them out of Thy hand. In Thy pitiful mercy let our remembrance reach them and comfort their hearts. For Thy love's sake.

• • •

O ALMIGHTY GOD, eternal treasure of all good things, never let my desires of this world be greedy, nor my thoughts intemperate, nor my cares vexatious and distracting; but moderate, holy, subordinate to Thy will, the measure Thou hast appointed me.

*Jeremy Taylor*

• • •

ALMIGHTY and everlasting God, the Comfort of the sad, the Strength of sufferers, let the prayers of those that cry out of any tribulation come unto Thee, that all may rejoice to find that Thy mercy is present with them in their afflictions.

*Fifth Century*

O MOST high, almighty, good Lord God, to Thee belong praise, glory, honor, and all blessing!

Praised be my Lord God with all His creatures, and specially our brother the sun, who brings us the day and who brings us the light; fair is he and shines with a very great splendor: O Lord, he signifies to us Thee!

Praised be my Lord for our sister the moon, and for the stars, the which He has set clear and lovely in heaven.

Praised be my Lord for our brother the wind, and for the air and cloud, calms and all weather by the which Thou upholdest life in all creatures.

Praised be my Lord for our sister water, who is very serviceable unto us and humble and precious and clean.

Praised be my Lord for our brother fire, through whom Thou givest us light in the darkness; and he is bright and pleasant and very mighty and strong.

Praised be my Lord for our mother the

earth, the which doth sustain us and keep us, and bringeth forth divers fruits and flowers of many colors, and grass.

Praised be my Lord for all those who pardon one another for His love's sake, and who endure weakness and tribulation; blessed are they who peaceably shall endure, for Thou, O most Highest, shalt give them a crown.

Praised be my Lord for our sister, the death of the body, from which no man escapeth. Woe to him who dieth in mortal sin! Blessed are they who are found walking by Thy most holy will, for the second death shall have no power to do them harm.

Praise ye and bless the Lord, and give thanks unto Him and serve Him with great humility.         *St. Francis of Assisi*

● ● ●

GRANT, O Lord, that we may live in Thy fear, die in Thy favor, rest in Thy peace, rise in Thy power, reign in Thy glory.
*Archbishop Laud*

MAY I be no man's enemy, and may I be the friend of that which is eternal and abides. May I never quarrel with those nearest me; and if I do, may I be reconciled quickly. May I never devise evil against any man; if any devise evil against me, may I escape uninjured and without the need of hurting him. May I love, seek, and attain only that which is good. May I wish for all men's happiness and envy none. May I never rejoice in the ill-fortune of one who has wronged me. When I have done or said what is wrong, may I never wait for the rebuke of others, but always rebuke myself until I make amends.

*Eusebius*

● ● ●

O THOU who art Love, and who seest all the suffering, injustice and misery which reign in this world; look mercifully upon the poor, the oppressed, and all who are heavy laden with labor and sorrow. Fill our hearts with deep compassion for those who suffer, and hasten the coming of Thy kingdom of justice and truth.

● ● ●

O LORD, who hast given us Thy summer sun to gladden us with his light and to ripen the fruits of the earth for our support, and who biddest him to set when his work is done, that he may rise again to-morrow; give Thy blessing to us Thy servants, that the lesson of the works of Thy hand may be learnt by us Thy living works, and that we may run our course like the sun which is now gone from us.

Let us rise early and go late to rest, being ever busy and zealous in doing Thy will. Let our light shine before men, that they may glorify Thee, our Heavenly Father. Let us do good all our days, and be useful to and comfort others. And let us finish our course in faith, that we too may rise again to a course which shall never end.

*Thomas Arnold*

●   ●   ●

O GOD, that bringest all things to pass, grant me the spirit of reverence for noble things. May I walk in the guileless paths of life, and leave behind me a fair name for my children.     *Pindar*

11

BESTOW on me, O Lord, a genial spirit and unwearied forbearance; a mild, loving, patient heart; kindly looks, pleasant, cordial speech and manners in the intercourse of daily life; that I may give offense to none, but as much as in me lies, live in charity with all men.      *Johann Arndt*

• • •

ALMIGHTY and everlasting God, Who art always more ready to hear than we to pray, and art wont to give more than either we desire or deserve, pour down upon us the abundance of Thy mercy, forgiving us those things whereof our conscience is afraid, and giving us those things which we are not worthy to ask.

*Leonine Sacramentary*

• • •

O LORD, give us all, we beseech Thee, grace and strength to overcome every sin; sins of besetment, deliberation, surprise, negligence, omission; sins against Thee, our self, our neighbor; sins great, small, remembered, forgotten.      *Christina Rossetti*

12

LORD, I know not what I ought to ask of Thee; Thou only knowest what I need. Thou lovest me better than I know how to love myself. O Father, give to Thy child that which he himself knows not how to ask.

I simply present myself before Thee; I open my heart to Thee. Behold my needs which I know not myself; see, and do according to Thy tender mercy. Smite, or heal; depress me, or raise me up. I adore all Thy purposes without knowing them; I am silent, I offer myself in sacrifice, I yield myself to Thee.

I would have no other desire than to accomplish Thy will. Teach me to pray; pray Thyself in me.          *François Fénelon*

•　•　•

O GOD, who tellest the number of the stars, and callest them all by their names; heal, we beseech Thee, the contrite in heart, and gather together the outcasts, and enrich us with the fullness of Thy wisdom.          *Sarum Breviary*

14

LORD, I am no hero, I have been careless, cowardly, sometimes all but mutinous. Punishment I have deserved, I deny it not. But a traitor I have never been; a deserter I have never been. I have tried to fight on Thy side in Thy battle against evil.

I have tried to do the duty which lay nearest me; and to leave whatever Thou didst commit to my charge a little better than I found it.

I have not been good, but at least I have tried to be good. Take the will for the deed, good Lord.

Strike not my unworthy name off the roll-call . . . even though I stand lowest and last upon the list.　*Charles Kingsley*

● ● ●

SPEAK, Lord, for Thy servant heareth. Grant us ears to hear, eyes to see, wills to obey, hearts to love; then declare what Thou wilt, reveal what Thou wilt, command what Thou wilt, demand what Thou wilt.

*Christina Rossetti*

15

O Lord, who art as the shadow of a great rock in a weary land, who beholdest Thy weak creatures, weary of labor, weary of pleasure, weary of hope deferred, weary of self, in Thine abundant compassion and unutterable tenderness, bring us unto Thy rest.                    *Christina Rossetti*

●  ●  ●

O my Lord! If I worship Thee from fear of hell, burn me in hell; and if I worship Thee from hope of paradise, exclude me thence; but if I worship Thee for Thine own sake, then withhold not from me Thine Eternal Beauty.        *Moslem Prayer*

●  ●  ●

Lord, turn my necessities into virtue; the works of nature into the works of grace; by making them orderly, regular, temperate; and let no pride or self-seeking, no covetousness or revenge, no little ends and low imaginations, pollute my spirit, but let my body be a servant of my spirit, that, doing all things for Thy glory here, I may be partaker of Thy glory hereafter.

*Jeremy Taylor*

LORD, Thou knowest better than I know myself that I am growing older, and will some day be old.

Keep me from getting talkative, and particularly from the fatal habit of thinking I must say something on every subject and on every occasion.

Release me from craving to try to straighten out everybody's affairs.

Keep my mind free from the recital of endless details — give me wings to get to the point.

I ask for grace enough to listen to the tales of others' pains. Help me to endure them with patience.

But seal my lips on my own aches and pains — they are increasing and my love of rehearsing them is becoming sweeter as the years go by.

Teach me the glorious lesson that occasionally it is possible that I may be mistaken.

Keep me reasonably sweet; I do not want to be a saint — some of them are so hard

17

to live with — but a sour old woman is one of the crowning works of the devil.

Make me thoughtful, but not moody; helpful, but not bossy. With my vast store of wisdom, it seems a pity not to use it all — but Thou knowest, Lord, that I want a few friends at the end. *A Mother Superior who wishes to be anonymous*

● ● ●

O LORD, grant that each one who has to do with me today may be the happier for it. Let it be given me each hour today what I shall say, and grant me the wisdom of a loving heart that I may say the right thing rightly.

Help me to enter into the mind of everyone who talks with me, and keep me alive to the feelings of each one present. Give me a quick eye for little kindnesses that I may be ready in doing them and gracious in receiving them. Give me a quick perception of the feelings and needs of others, and make me eagerhearted in helping them.

● ● ●

O GOD of peace, we turn aside from an unquiet world, seeking rest for our spirits and light for our thoughts. We bring our work to be sanctified, our wounds to be healed, our sins to be forgiven, our hopes to be renewed, our better selves to be quickened. O Thou, in whom there is harmony, draw us to thyself, and silence the discords of our wasteful lives. Thou who art one in all, and in whom all are one, take us out of the loneliness of self, and fill us with the fullness of Thy truth and love. Thou whose greatness is beyond our highest praise, lift us above our common littleness and our daily imperfections; send us visions of the love that is in Thee and of the good that may be in us.

● ● ●

I THANK Thee, Lord, for knowing me better than I know myself, and for letting me know myself better than others know me.

Make me, I pray Thee, better than they suppose, and forgive me what they do not know.                    *Arabian*

19

MAY THE strength of God pilot us. May the power of God preserve us. May the wisdom of God instruct us. May the hand of God protect us. May the way of God direct us. May the shield of God defend us.

May the host of God guard us against the snares of the Evil One and the temptations of the world.                    *St. Patrick*

• • •

ALMIGHTY God, Lord of the storm and of the calm, the vexed sea and the quiet haven, of day and night, of life and of death; grant unto us so to have our hearts stayed upon Thy faithfulness, Thine unchangingness and love, that, whatsoever betide us, however black the cloud or dark the night, with quiet faith trusting in Thee, we may look upon Thee with untroubled eye, and walking in lowliness towards Thee, and in lovingness towards one another, abide all storms and troubles of this mortal life, beseeching Thee that they may turn to the soul's true good; we ask it for Thy mercy's sake.      *George Dawson*

I OFFER to Thee prayers for all those whom I have in any way grieved, vexed and oppressed, by word or deed, knowingly or unknowingly, that Thou mayest equally forgive us all our sins, and all our offenses against each other.

Take away, O Lord, from our hearts all suspiciousness, indignation, anger and contention, and whatever is likely to wound charity and to lessen brotherly love.

Have mercy, O Lord, have mercy on those who seek Thy mercy; give grace to the needy; make us so to live that we may be found worthy to enjoy the fruits of Thy grace.

*Thomas à Kempis*

●　●　●

O LORD, grant us to love Thee; grant that we may love those that love Thee; grant that we may do the deeds that win Thy love. Make the love of Thee to be dearer to us than ourselves, than our families, than wealth, and even than cool water.

*Mohammed*

22

GIVE us courage, gaiety and the quiet mind. Spare to us our friends, soften to us our enemies. Bless us, if it may be, in all our innocent endeavors. If it may not, give us the strength to encounter that which is to come, that we be brave in peril, constant in tribulation, temperate in wrath, and in all changes of fortune and down to the gates of death, loyal and loving one to another.

*Robert Louis Stevenson*

● ● ●

GRANT me, O Lord, to know what I ought to know, to love what I ought to love, to praise what delights Thee most, to value what is precious in Thy sight, to hate what is offensive to Thee.

Do not suffer me to judge according to the sight of my eyes, nor to pass sentence according to the hearing of the ears of ignorant men; but to discern with a true judgment between things visible and spiritual, and above all things always to inquire what is the good pleasure of Thy will.

*Thomas à Kempis*

23

KEEP us this night, O Lord, from all works of darkness, and whether we wake or sleep, let our thoughts and deeds be in accordance with Thy holy will. Preserve us from all dangers and terrors of the night; from restless watching and sorrowful thoughts; from unnecessary or fretful care and imaginary fears. Let us awake tomorrow renewed in strength, and cheerful in spirit; may we arise with holy thoughts, and go forth to live to Thine honor, to the service of our fellowmen, and the comfort and joy of our households.

*Caspar Neumann*

• • •

O LORD, the Lord whose ways are right, keep us in Thy mercy from lip-service and empty forms; from having a name that we live, but being dead.

Help us to worship Thee by righteous deeds and lives of holiness; that our prayer also may be set forth in Thy sight as the incense, and the lifting up of our hands be as an evening sacrifice.

*Christina Rossetti*

O GOD, make the door of this house wide enough to receive all who need human love and fellowship, narrow enough to shut out all envy, pride and strife.

Make its threshold smooth enough to be no stumbling-block to children, nor to straying feet, but rugged and strong enough to turn back the tempter's power. God make the door of this house the gateway to Thine eternal kingdom.

*Door of St. Stephen's, London*

● ● ●

ALMIGHTY God, comfort us by Thy fullness. Our strength is but weakness, our knowledge is but small, our life but passing away. By Thine eternal wisdom, by Thine unshaken power, Thy constant years, Thine unfailing love, uphold and comfort us, that we, ever feeling that our little lives are altogether in Thee, may look forward to the ending of this mortal life without fear, longing for and hoping for an entrance into that large abundant life where Thou shalt be all in all.

*George Dawson*

25

O LORD, our heavenly Father, Almighty and everlasting God, who hast safely brought us to the beginning of this day; defend us in the same with Thy mighty power; and grant that this day we fall into no sin, neither run into any kind of danger; but that all our doings, being ordered by Thy governance, may be righteous in Thy sight.

*Book of Common Prayer*

• • •

I NEED Thee to teach me day by day, according to each day's opportunities and needs. Give me, O my Lord, that purity of conscience which alone can receive, which alone can improve Thy inspirations.

My ears are dull, so that I cannot hear Thy voice. My eyes are dim, so that I cannot see Thy token. Thou alone canst quicken my hearing, and purge my sight, and cleanse and renew my heart.

Teach me to sit at Thy feet, and to hear Thy word.

*John Henry Newman*

LORD, though I am a miserable and wretched creature, I am in Covenant with Thee through grace. And I may, I will, come to Thee, for Thy People. Thou hast made me, though very unworthy, a mean instrument to do them some good, and Thee service; and many of them have set too high a value upon me, though others wish and would be glad of my death; Lord, however Thou dost dispose of me, continue and go on to do good for them. Give them consistency of judgment, one heart, and mutual love. Teach those who look too much on Thy instruments, to depend more upon Thyself. Pardon such as desire to trample upon the dust of a poor worm, for they are Thy people too. And pardon the folly of this short Prayer.

*Oliver Cromwell*

●  ●  ●

GRANT me grace to desire ardently all that is pleasing to Thee, to examine it prudently, to acknowledge it truthfully, and to accomplish it perfectly, for the praise and glory of Thy name.    *Thomas Aquinas*

O LORD God everlasting, Which reignest over the kingdoms of men, so teach me I humbly beseech Thee, Thy word, and so strengthen me with Thy grace that I may feed Thy people with a faithful and a true heart, and rule them prudently with power. O Lord, Thou hast set me on high. My flesh is frail and weak. If I therefore at any time forget Thee, touch my heart, O Lord, that I may again remember Thee. If I swell against Thee, pluck me down in my own conceit. . . . I acknowledge, O my King, without Thee my throne is unstable, my seat unsure, my kingdom tottering, my life uncertain. I see all things in this life subject to mutability, nothing to continue still at one stay. Create therefore in me, O Lord, a new heart, and so renew my spirit that Thy law may be my study, Thy Truth my delight, Thy church my care, Thy people my crown, Thy righteousness my pleasure, Thy service my government; so shall this my kingdom through Thee be established with peace.

*Queen Elizabeth I*

GRANT unto us, Almighty God, the peace of God that passeth understanding, that we, amid the storms and troubles of this our life, may rest in Thee, knowing that all things are in Thee; not beneath Thine eye only, but under Thy care, governed by Thy will, guarded by Thy love, so that with a quiet heart we may see the storms of life, the cloud and the thick darkness, ever rejoicing to know that the darkness and the light are both alike to Thee. Guide, guard, and govern us even to the end, that none of us may fail to lay hold upon the immortal life.

*George Dawson*

●　●　●

WE ARE evil, O God, and help us to see it and amend. We are good, and help us to be better. Look down upon Thy servants with a patient eye, even as Thou sendest sun and rain; look down, call upon the dry bones, quicken, enliven; recreate in us the soul of service, the spirit of peace; renew in us the sense of joy.

*Robert Louis Stevenson*

30

IN THE name of God, the Giver, Forgiver, rich in love, praise be to the name of Ormazd, the God who always was, always is, and always will be; the heavenly among the heavenly, with the name "From whom alone is the law derived."

With all strength bring I thanks. All good do I accept at Thy command, O God, and think, and speak, and do it. I believe in the pure law; by every good work I seek forgiveness for all sins. I keep pure the six powers — thought, speech, work, memory, mind, and understanding. According to Thy will I am able to accomplish, O accomplisher of good, Thy honor with good thoughts and good works.

Praise be to the Overseer, the Lord, who rewards those who accomplish good deeds according to His own wish, and at last purifies even the wicked ones of hell.

*Persian*

● ● ●

O LORD, Thou knowest how busy I must be this day. If I forget Thee, do not Thou forget me. *Jacob Astley*

31

O THOU full of compassion, I commit and commend myself unto Thee, in whom I am, and live, and know. Be Thou the Goal of my pilgrimage, and my Rest by the way. Let my soul take refuge from the crowding turmoil of worldly thought beneath the shadow of Thy wings; let my heart, this sea of restless waves, find peace in Thee, O God. *St. Augustine*

● ● ●

WE MUST praise Thy goodness, that Thou hast left nothing undone to draw us to Thyself. But one thing we ask of Thee, our God, not to cease Thy work in our improvement. Let us tend towards Thee, no matter by what means, and be fruitful in good works. *Ludwig van Beethoven*

● ● ●

O FATHER, light up the small duties of this day's life: may they shine with the beauty of Thy countenance. May we believe that glory can dwell in the commonest task of every day. *St. Augustine*

FATHER, let me hold Thy hand, and like a child walk with Thee down all my days, secure in Thy love and strength.

*Thomas à Kempis*

• • •

O MERCIFUL God, be Thou unto me a strong tower of defense, I humbly entreat Thee. Give me grace to await Thy leisure, and patiently to bear what Thou doest unto me; nothing doubting or mistrusting Thy goodness towards me, for Thou knowest what is good for me better than I do. Therefore do with me in all things what Thou wilt; only arm me, I beseech Thee, with Thine armor, that I may stand fast; above all things, taking to me the shield of faith; praying always that I may refer myself wholly to Thy will, abiding Thy pleasure, and comforting myself in those troubles which it shall please Thee to send me, seeing such troubles are profitable for me; and I am assuredly persuaded that all Thou doest cannot but be well; and unto Thee be all honor and glory.

*Lady Jane Grey*

33

O LORD God, when Thou givest to Thy
servants to endeavor any great matter,
grant us also to know that it is not the beginning, but the continuing of the same
until it be thoroughly finished, which
yieldeth the true glory.      *Francis Drake*

•   •   •

BLESS all who worship Thee, from the ris-
ing of the sun unto the going down of the
same. Of Thy goodness, give us; with Thy
love, inspire us; by Thy spirit, guide us;
by Thy power, protect us; in Thy mercy
receive us now and always.

*Ancient Collect*

•   •   •

GRANT, O Father, to our minds, to climb
to that august abode, grant us to visit the
Fountain of the Good, grant that, finding
the Light, we may open wide and fix on
Thee the eyes of our souls. Scatter the
mists and heaviness of the earthly mass,
and shine out with Thy own splendor: for
Thou art the Serene.      *Boethius*

In Thee, O Lord God, I place my whole hope and refuge; on Thee I rest all my tribulation and anguish; for I find all to be weak and inconstant, whatsoever I behold out of Thee. For many friends cannot profit, nor strong helpers assist, nor the books of the learned afford comfort, nor any place, however retired and lonely, give shelter, unless Thou Thyself dost assist, strengthen, console, instruct, and guard us. For all things that seem to belong to the attainment of peace and felicity, without Thee, are nothing, and do bring in truth no felicity at all. Thou therefore art the Fountain of all that is good; and to hope in Thee above all things is the strongest comfort of Thy servants. To Thee, therefore, do I lift up mine eyes; in Thee, my God, the Father of mercies, do I put my trust. *Thomas à Kempis*

●  ●  ●

I will whatsoever Thou willest; I will because Thou willest; I will in that manner Thou willest; I will as long as Thou willest. *F. B. Meyer*

O LORD, support us all the day long, until the shadows lengthen and the evening comes, and the busy world is hushed, and the fever of life is over, and our work is done. Then in Thy mercy grant us a safe lodging, and a holy rest, and peace at the last. *Sixteenth Century*

• • •

UNTO God's gracious mercy and protection we commit ourselves. The Lord bless us and keep us. The Lord make His face to shine upon us and be gracious unto us. The Lord lift up the light of His countenance upon us, and give us peace, both now and evermore. *Numbers 6:24-26*

• • •

LORD, may I be wakeful at sunrise to begin a new day for Thee, cheerful at sunset for having done my work for Thee; thankful at moonrise and under starshine for the beauty of Thy universe. And may I add what little may be in me to add to Thy great world. *Abbot of Grève*

36

WE THANK Thee, Lord, for the glory of the late days and the excellent face of Thy sun. We thank Thee for good news received. We thank Thee for the pleasures we have enjoyed and for those we have been able to confer. And now, when the clouds gather and the rain impends, permit us not to be cast down; let us not lose the savor of past mercies and past pleasures; but, like the voice of a bird singing in the rain, let grateful memory survive in the hour of darkness. If there be in front of us any painful duty, strengthen us with the grace of courage; if any act of mercy, teach us tenderness and patience.

*Robert Louis Stevenson*

●　　●　　●

O LORD our God, when the storm is loud, and the night is dark, and the soul is sad, and the heart oppressed; then, as weary travelers, may we look to Thee; and beholding the light of Thy love, may it bear us on, until we learn to sing Thy song in the night.　　*George Dawson*

ALMIGHTY Father, Source of all blessings, we thank Thee for the preservation of our life and for the joy of living, for the powers of mind and heart and for the wisdom that comes to us from seers and sages filled with Thy spirit.

Teach us to use wisely the blessings Thou hast bestowed upon us. May prosperity not enfeeble our spirit nor harden our heart. May it never so master us as to dull our desire for life's higher ideals.

And should adversity come, may it not embitter us nor cause us to despair, but may we accept it as a mark of Thy chastening love which purifies and strengthens. Let every obstacle become an incentive to greater effort, and let every defeat teach us anew the lesson of patience and perseverance.

Gird us with strength to bear our trials with courage. Let not the loss of anything, however dear to our hearts or precious in our sight, rob us of our faith in Thee. In light as in darkness, in joy as in sorrow, help us to put our trust in Thy providence, that even through our tears we may discern Thy divine blessing.

*Union Prayer Book*

●　●　●

I know, O Lord, and do with all humility acknowledge myself an object altogether unworthy of Thy love; but sure I am, Thou art an object altogether worthy of mine. I am not good enough to serve Thee, but Thou hast a right to my best service.

Do Thou then impart to me some of that excellence, and that shall supply my own want of worth. Help me to cease from sin according to Thy will, that I may be capable of doing Thee service according to my duty.

Enable me so to guard and govern myself, so to begin and finish my course that, when the race of life is run, I may sleep in peace and rest in Thee.

Be with me unto the end, that my sleep may be rest indeed, my rest perfect security, and that security a blessed eternity.

*St. Augustine*

O GOD, who hast commanded us to be perfect, as Thou art perfect; put into my heart, I pray Thee, a continual desire to obey Thy holy will. Teach me day by day what Thou wouldst have me to do, and give me grace and power to fulfill the same. May I never, from love of ease, decline the path which Thou pointest out, nor, for fear of shame, turn away from it.

*Henry Allford*

•  •  •

BE PLEASED, O Lord, to remember my friends, all that have prayed for me, and all that have done me good.

Do Thou good to them and return all their kindness double into their own bosom, rewarding them with blessings, and sanctifying them with Thy graces, and bringing them to glory.

Let all my family and kindred, my neighbors and acquaintances receive the benefit of my prayers, and the blessings of God; the comforts and supports of Thy providence, and the sanctification of Thy Spirit.

*Jeremy Taylor*

41

BRING us, O Lord God, at our last awakening into the house and gate of heaven, to enter into that gate and dwell in that house, where there shall be no darkness nor dazzling, but one equal light; no noise nor silence, but one equal music; no fears nor hopes, but one equal possession; no ends nor beginnings, but one equal eternity; in the habitations of Thy glory and dominion world without end.

*John Donne*

•   •   •

O GOD, the physician of men and nations, the restorer of the years that have been destroyed; look upon the distractions of the world, and be pleased to complete the work of Thy healing hand; draw all men unto Thee and one to another by the bands of Thy love; make Thy Church one, and fill it with Thy Spirit, that by That power it may unite the world in a sacred brotherhood of nations, wherein justice, mercy and faith, truth and freedom may flourish, and Thou mayest be ever glorified.

*Acts of Devotion*

42

GOD of our life, there are days when the burdens we carry chafe our shoulders and weigh us down; when the road seems dreary and endless, the skies grey and threatening; when our lives have no music in them, and our hearts are lonely, and our souls have lost their courage. Flood the path with light, we beseech Thee; turn our eyes to where the skies are full of promise; tune our hearts to brave music; give us the sense of comradeship with heroes and saints of every age; and so quicken our spirits that we may be able to encourage the souls of all who journey with us on the road of life, to Thy honor and glory.                     *St. Augustine*

● ● ●

O GOD, by Thy mercy strengthen us who lie exposed to the rough storms of troubles and temptations. Help us against our own negligence and cowardice, and defend us from the treachery of our unfaithful hearts. Succor us, we beseech Thee, and bring us to Thy safe haven of peace and felicity.                     *Thomas à Kempis*

43

WHEN I behold the problems of our world, O Lord, I pray not to be tempted to quick answers. When every tongue declares a different Truth, when every people praises its own Righteousness, let me pause before I speak or praise or hope. Let me look inward seeking to discover eternal truths implanted there by Thee, truths greater than those heard in the outer multitude of voices and of words. And let me remember always that to be loud is not to be right, to be strange is not to be forbidden, to be new is not to be frightful, to be black is not to be ugly. Thus let me find truths true to Thee, that I may live with them, and Thee, and myself, in peace.

●　●　●

INTO Thy hands, O God, we commend ourselves, and all who are dear to us, this day. Let the gift of Thy special presence be with us even to its close. Grant us never to lose sight of Thee all the day long, but to worship, and pray to Thee, that at eventide we may again give thanks unto Thee.

*Gelasian Sacramentary*

WE BESEECH Thee, our most gracious God, preserve us from the cares of this life, lest we should be too much entangled therein; also from the many necessities of the body, lest we should be ensnared by pleasure; and from whatsoever is an obstacle to the soul, lest, being broken with troubles, we should be overthrown. Give us strength to resist, patience to endure, and constancy to persevere.

*Thomas à Kempis*

● ● ●

LET ME not seek out of Thee what I can find only in Thee, O Lord, peace and rest and joy and bliss, which abide only in Thine abiding joy. Lift up my soul above the weary round of harassing thoughts to Thy eternal Presence. Lift up my soul to the pure, bright, serene, radiant atmosphere of Thy Presence, that there I may breathe freely, there repose in Thy love, there be at rest from myself, and from all things that weary me; and thence return, arrayed with Thy peace, to do and bear what shall please Thee. *E. B. Pusey*

WE COME before Thee, O Lord, in the end of Thy day with thanksgiving.

Our beloved in the far parts of earth, those who are now beginning the labors of the day what time we end them, and those with whom the sun now stands at the point of noon, bless, help, console, and prosper them.

Our guard is relieved, the service of the day is over, and the hour come to rest. We resign into Thy hands our sleeping bodies, our cold hearths and open doors. Give us to awaken with smiles, give us to labor smiling. As the sun returns in the east, so let our patience be renewed with dawn; as the sun lightens the world, so let our loving kindness make bright his house of our habitation.           *Robert Louis Stevenson*

● ● ●

O GOD, our Refuge in pain, our Strength in weakness, our Help in trouble, we come to Thee in our hour of need, beseeching Thee to have mercy upon this Thine afflicted servant. O loving Father, relieve his pain. Yet if he needs must suffer,

47

strengthen him, that he may bear his sufferings with patience and as his day is, so may his strength be. Let not his heart be troubled, but shed down upon him the peace which passeth understanding. Though now for a season, if need be, he is in heaviness through his manifold trials, yet comfort him, O Lord, in all his sorrows, and let his mourning be turned into joy, and his sickness into health.

*E. B. Pusey*

•  •  •

LORD, take my lips and speak through them; take my mind, and think through it; take my heart, and set it on fire.

*W. H. Aitken*

•  •  •

O GOD, who knowest all things in earth and heaven, so fill my heart with trust in Thee, that by night and by day, at all times and in all seasons, I may, without fear, commit those who are dear to me to Thy never-failing love, for this life and the life to come.

•  •  •

THE DAY returns and brings us the petty round of irritating concerns and duties. Help us to play the man, help us to perform them with laughter and kind faces. Let cheerfulness abound with industry. Give us to go blithely on our business all this day, bring us to our resting-beds weary and content and undishonored, and grant us in the end the gift of sleep.

*Robert Louis Stevenson*

● ● ●

GOD grant me the serenity to accept the things I cannot change, the courage to change the things I can, and the wisdom to distinguish the one from the other.

*Reinhold Niebuhr*

● ● ●

TEACH us, good Lord, to serve Thee as Thou deservest; to give and not to count the cost; to fight and not to heed the wounds; to toil and not to seek for rest; to labor and not to ask for any reward, save that of knowing that we do Thy will.

*Ignatius Loyola*

49

O GOD of peace, we turn aside from an unquiet world, seeking rest for our spirits, and light for our thoughts. We bring our work to be sanctified, our wounds to be healed, our sins to be forgiven, our hopes to be renewed, our better selves to be quickened. O Thou, in whom there is harmony, draw us to Thyself, and silence the discords of our wasteful lives. Thou in whom all are one, take us out of the loneliness of self, and fill us with the fullness of Thy truth and love. Thou whose greatness is beyond our praise, lift us above our littleness and our daily imperfections; send us visions of the love that is in Thee and of the good that may be in us.

•  •  •

O GOD, though our sins be seven, though our sins be seventy times seven, though our sins be more in number than the hairs of our head, yet give us grace in loving penitence to cast ourselves down into the depths of Thy compassion.

*Christina Rossetti*

O GOD, keep my tongue from evil and my lips from speaking guile. Be my support when grief silences my voice, and my comfort when woe bends my spirit. Plant humility in my soul, and strengthen my heart with perfect faith in Thee. Help me to be strong in trial and temptation and to be meek when others wrong me, that I may readily forgive them. Guide me by the light of Thy counsel, and let me ever find rest in Thee, who are my Rock and my Redeemer. Let the words of my mouth and the meditation of my heart be acceptable in Thy sight, O Lord, my Rock and my Redeemer.     *Union Prayer Book*

●　●　●

O LORD, be gracious unto us! In all that we hear or see, in all that we say or do, be gracious unto us. I ask pardon of the Great God. I ask pardon at the sunset, when every sinner turns to Him. Now and for ever I ask pardon of God. O Lord, cover us from our sins, guard our children and protect our weaker friends.

*Camel-Driver's Prayer*

51

LORD, make me an instrument of Thy
    peace:
Where there is hatred, let me sow love;
Where there is injury, pardon;
Where there is discord, union;
Where there is doubt, faith;
Where there is despair, hope;
Where there is darkness, light;
Where there is sadness, joy.

O Divine Master, grant that I may not
    so much seek
To be consoled, as to console;
To be understood, as to understand;
To be loved, as to love;
For it is in giving that we receive,
It is in pardoning that we are pardoned,
And it is in dying that we are born
To Eternal Life.

*St. Francis of Assisi*

● ● ●

GOD give me work
Till my life shall end
And life
Till my work is done.

*Yorkshire Tombstone*

O GOD our Father, on this Day of Remembrance, look upon the unrest of the world and be pleased to complete the work of Thy healing hand. Send peace upon the earth, a deeper and more lasting peace than the world has ever known. Draw all men unto Thyself, and to one another by the bands of love. Grant understanding to the Nations with an increase of sympathy and mutual good will, that they may be united in a sacred Brotherhood wherein justice, mercy and faith, truth and freedom may flourish, so that the sacrifice of those who died may not have been made in vain.

● ● ●

OUR FATHER, who art in heaven, hallowed be Thy name. Thy kingdom come. Thy will be done on earth, as it is in heaven. Give us this day our daily bread. And forgive us our trespasses, as we forgive those who trespass against us. And lead us not into temptation; but deliver us from evil: for Thine is the kingdom, and the power, and the glory, for ever and ever.

● ● ●

O Lord, renew our spirits and draw our hearts unto Thyself, that our work may not be to us a burden, but a delight; and give us such a mighty love to Thee as may sweeten all our obedience. Oh, let us not serve Thee with the spirit of bondage as slaves, but with cheerfulness and the gladness of children, delighting ourselves in Thee, and rejoicing in Thy work.

*Benjamin Jenks*

● ● ●

Give me, O Lord, a steadfast heart, which no unworthy affection may drag downwards; give me an unconquered heart, which no tribulation can wear out; give me an upright heart, which no unworthy purpose may tempt aside.

*Thomas Aquinas*

● ● ●

God be in my head, and in my understanding; God be in my eyes, and in my looking; God be in my mouth, and in my speaking; God be in my heart, and in my thinking; God be at my end, and at my departing.

*Old Sarum Primer*

55

O GOD, help me to think of Thee in this bitter trial. Thou knowest how my heart is rent with grief. In my weakness, tested so severely in soul by this visitation, I cry unto Thee, Father of all life: give me fortitude to say with Thy servant Job: "The Lord hath given; the Lord hath taken away; blessed be the name of the Lord."

Forgive the thoughts of my rebellious soul. Pardon me in these first hours of my grief, if I question Thy wisdom and exercise myself in things too high for me. Grant me strength to rise above this trial, to bear with humility life's sorrows and disappointments. Be nigh unto me, O God. Bring consolation and peace to my soul. Praised art Thou, O God, who comfortest the mourners.

*Union Prayer Book*

• • •

GRANT us grace to rest from all sinful deeds and thoughts, to surrender ourselves wholly unto Thee, and to keep our souls still before Thee like a still lake; that so the beams of Thy grace may be mirrored

56

therein, and may kindle in our hearts the glow of faith, and love, and prayer. May we, through such stillness and hope, find strength and gladness in Thee, O God, now and for evermore.    *Joachim Embden*

• • •

O THOU who art Love, and who seest all the suffering, injustice and misery which reign in this world; look mercifully upon the poor, the oppressed, and all who are heavy laden with labor and sorrow. Fill our hearts with deep compassion for those who suffer, help us to help them in the hour of their extremity, and hasten the coming of Thy blessed kingdom of justice and truth.

• • •

O GOD, be merciful to all who groan under the bondage of their sins, and show Thy grace to those who are burdened with the memory of their offenses; that, as not one of us is free from fault, so not one may be shut out from pardon.

*Gelasian Sacramentary*

O BLESSED Lord, I beseech Thee to pour down upon me such grace as may not only cleanse this life of mine, but beautify it a little, if it be Thy will, before I go hence and am no more seen. Grant that I may love Thee with all my heart and soul and mind and strength, and my neighbor as myself — and that I may persevere unto the end.

*James Skinner*

•   •   •

TAKE, O Lord, and receive my entire liberty, my memory, my understanding, and my whole will. All that I am, all that I have, Thou hast given me, and I will give it back again to Thee to be disposed of according to Thy good pleasure. Give me only Thy love and Thy grace; with Thee I am rich enough, nor do I ask for aught besides.

*Ignatius Loyola*

•   •   •

GIVE me, O Lord, a tender conscience, a conversation discreet and affable, modest and patient, liberal and obliging; a body chaste and healthful, competency of liv-

ing according to my condition, contentedness in all estates, a resigned will and
mortified affections; that I may be as Thou
wouldest have me, and my portion may
be in the lot of the righteous, in the bright-
ness of Thy countenance, and the glories
of eternity.                    *Jeremy Taylor*

• • •

LORD, behold our family here assembled.
We thank Thee for this place in which
we dwell; for the love that unites us; for
the peace accorded us this day; for the
hope with which we expect the morrow;
for the health, the work, the food and the
bright skies that make our lives delight-
ful; for our friends in all parts of the earth,
and our friendly helpers in this foreign
isle.                    *Robert Louis Stevenson*

• • •

WRITE Thy blessed name, O Lord, upon
my heart, there to remain so engraven that
no prosperity, no adversity, shall ever
move me from Thy love.
                    *Thomas à Kempis*

59

FORGIVE me, most gracious Lord and Father, if this day I have done or said anything to increase the pain of the world. Pardon the unkind word, the impatient gesture, the hard and selfish deed, the failure to show sympathy and kindly help where I had the opportunity, but missed it; and enable me so to live that I may daily do something to lessen the tide of human sorrow, and add to the sum of human happiness.        *F. B. Meyer*

• • •

O GOD, animate us to cheerfulness. May we have a joyful sense of our blessings, learn to look on the bright circumstances of our lot, and maintain a perpetual contentedness. Preserve us from despondency and from yielding to dejection. Teach us that nothing can hurt us if, with true loyalty of affection, we keep Thy commandments and take refuge in Thee.
        *William E. Channing*

• • •

LORD, teach us to pray.        *Luke* xi. 1